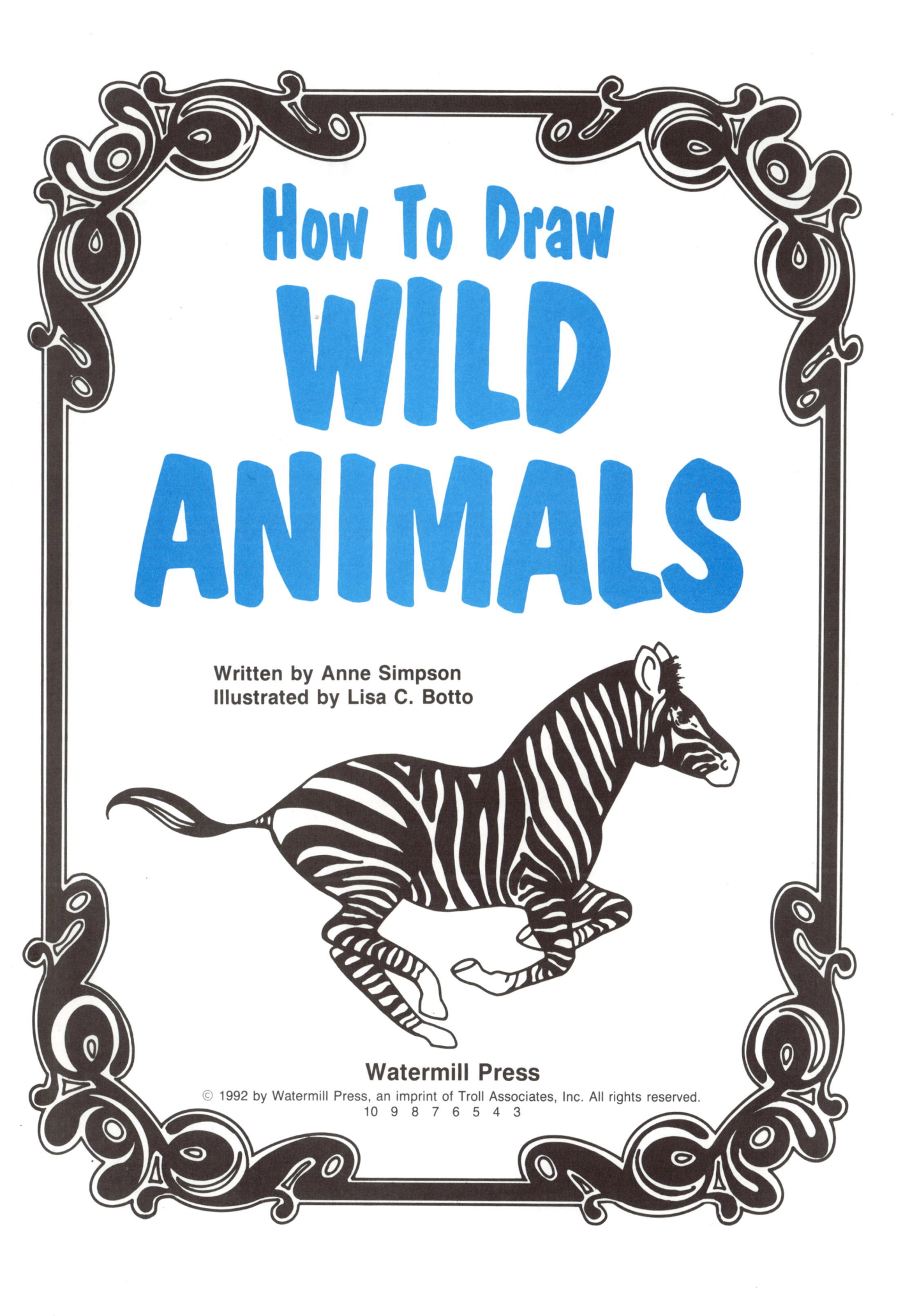

# How To Draw
# WILD ANIMALS

Written by Anne Simpson
Illustrated by Lisa C. Botto

**Watermill Press**

© 1992 by Watermill Press, an imprint of Troll Associates, Inc. All rights reserved.
10 9 8 7 6 5 4 3

# Introduction

Wild animals come in all shapes and sizes. They can be as small as a parrot, or as big as an elephant. Some are striped, some are spotted, and some have colors you wouldn't believe! Wild animals live in many different places—in the jungle, in the desert, and on the grassy plain.

Would you like to learn to draw some of these animals? It's easy when you follow the directions in this book. All you need are a few simple materials and a little imagination. Before you start to draw, you might want to trace a few of the basic animal shapes. But the most important thing to remember is—have fun!

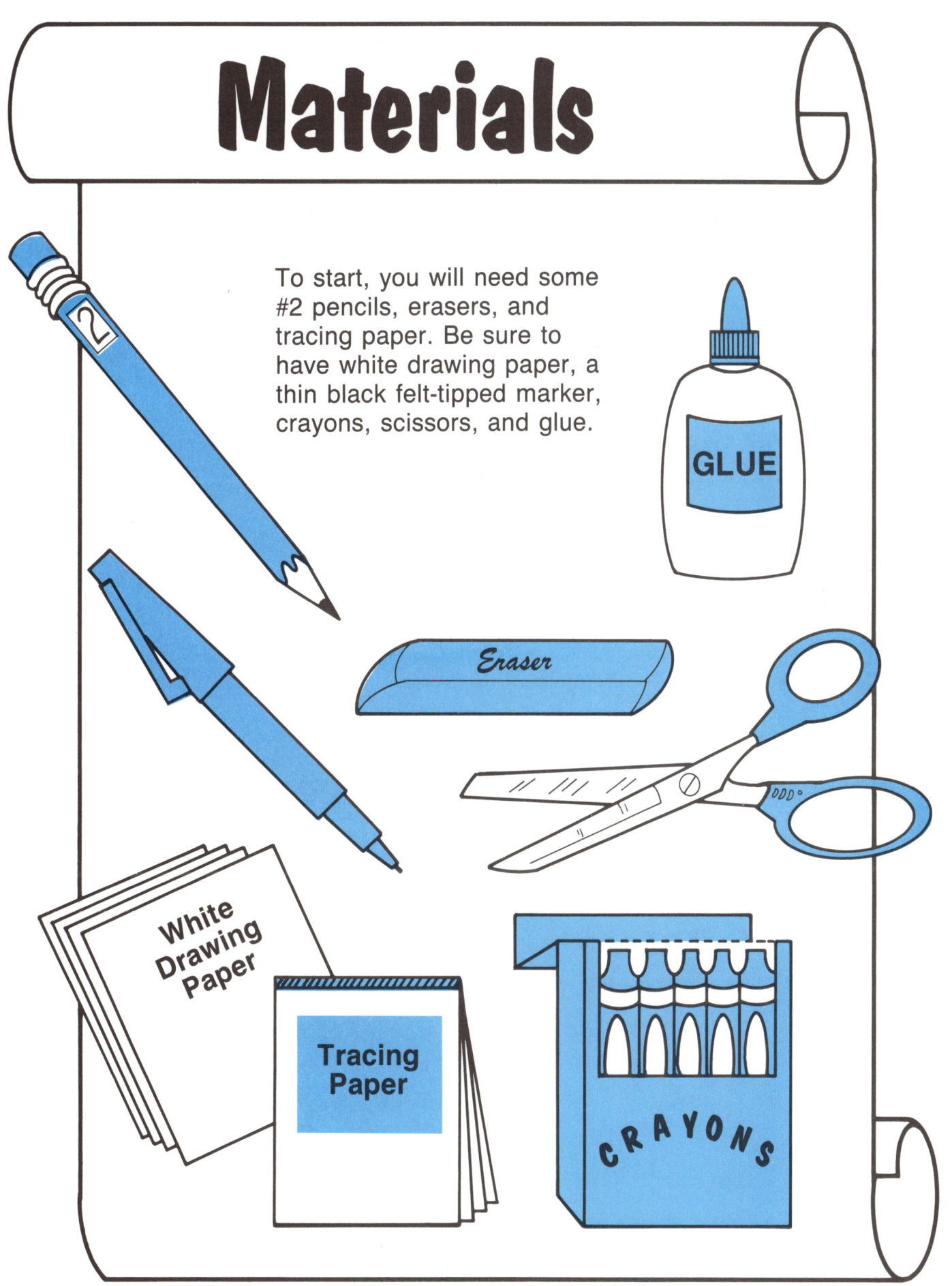

# Materials

To start, you will need some #2 pencils, erasers, and tracing paper. Be sure to have white drawing paper, a thin black felt-tipped marker, crayons, scissors, and glue.

# Elephant

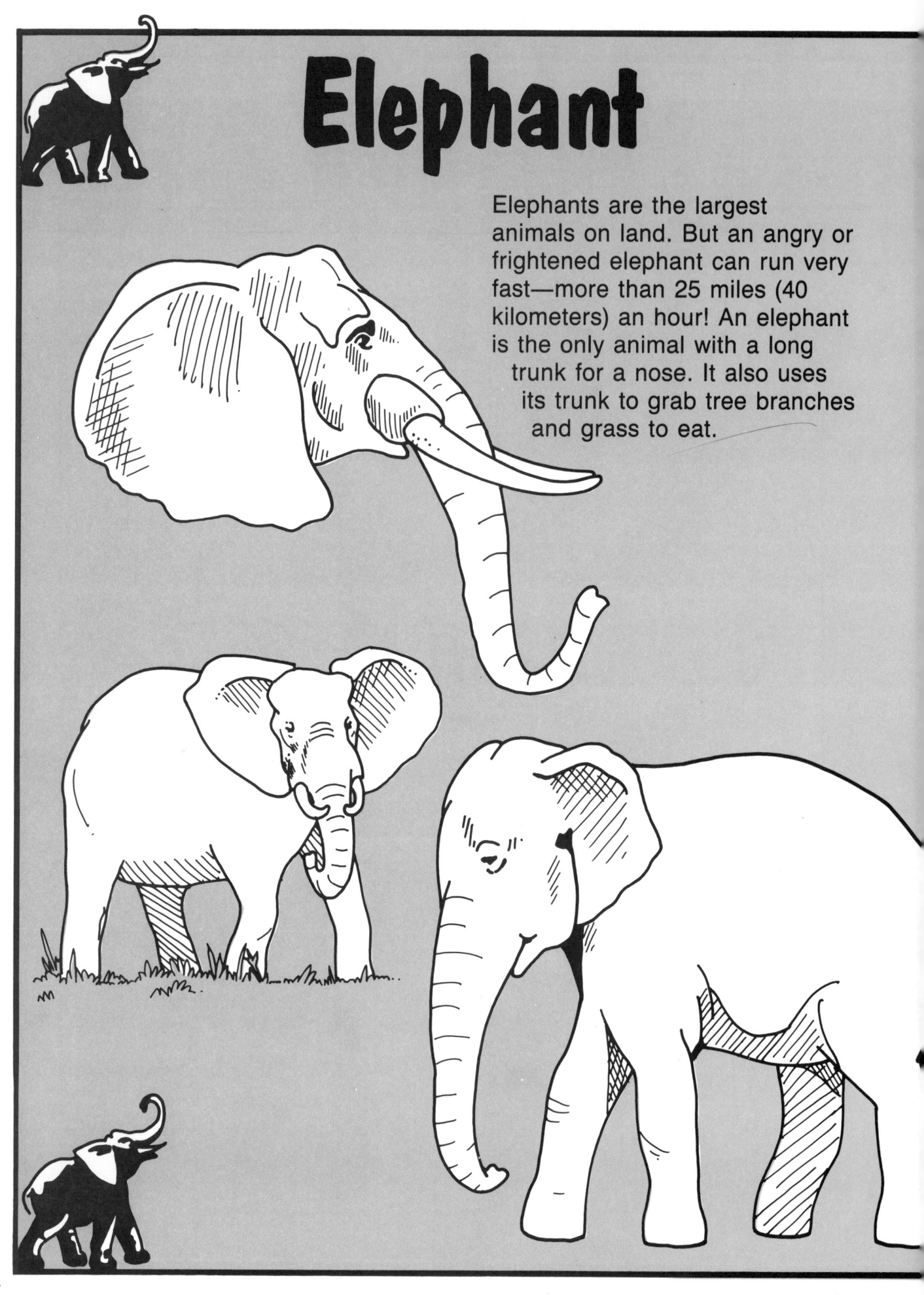

Elephants are the largest animals on land. But an angry or frightened elephant can run very fast—more than 25 miles (40 kilometers) an hour! An elephant is the only animal with a long trunk for a nose. It also uses its trunk to grab tree branches and grass to eat.

**1** Draw the basic body shapes.

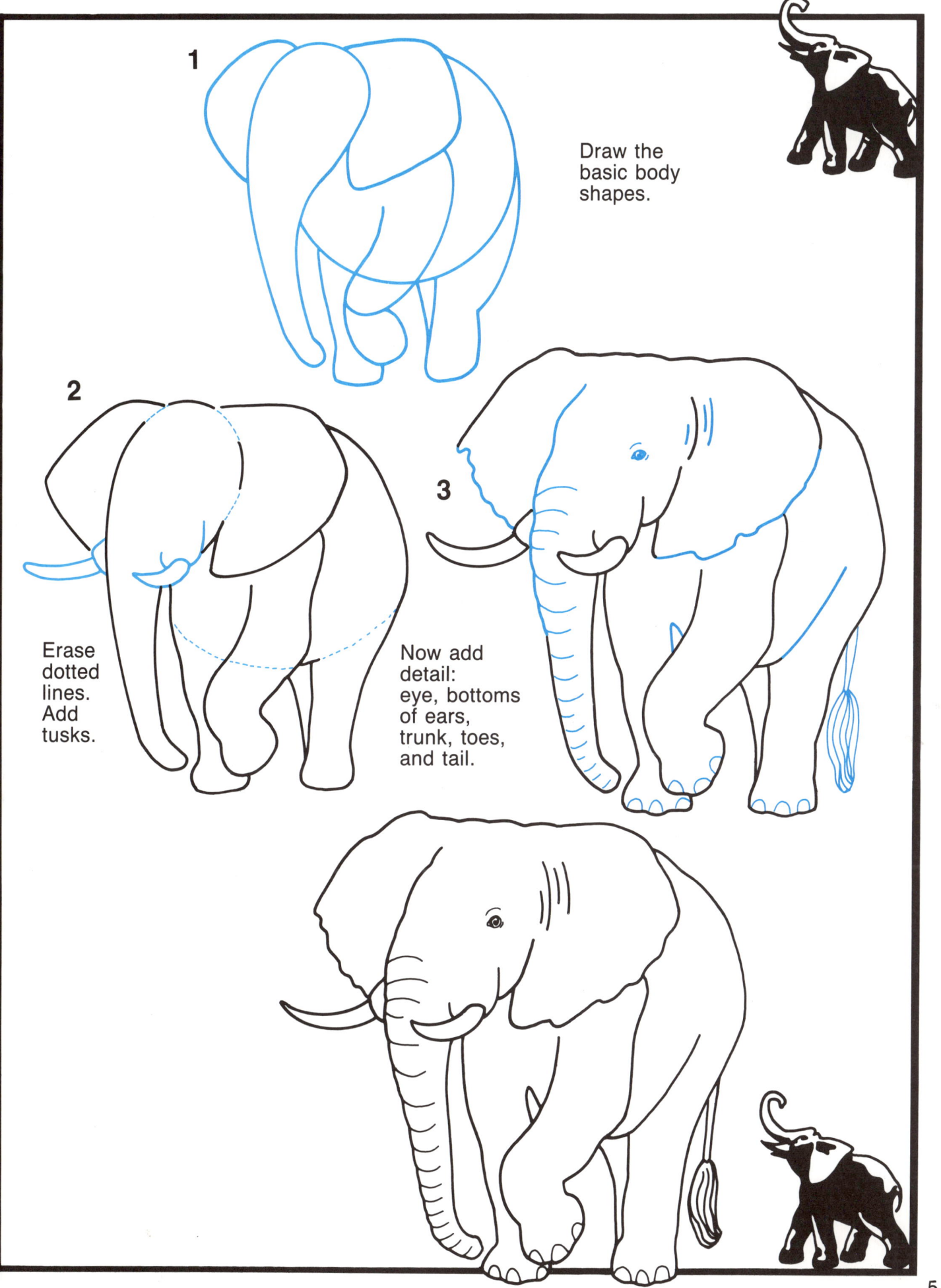

**2** Erase dotted lines. Add tusks.

**3** Now add detail: eye, bottoms of ears, trunk, toes, and tail.

# Monkey

The monkey family includes baboons, monkeys, and marmosets. The chacma baboon has grayish-brown fur and a ruff, or collar of hair, around its neck. The spider monkey got its name because it looks like a spider when it hangs upside down from a branch. It often hangs by its tail, and can swing quickly through the trees.

**Spider Monkey**

**Chacma Baboon**

**1** Draw the basic body shapes.

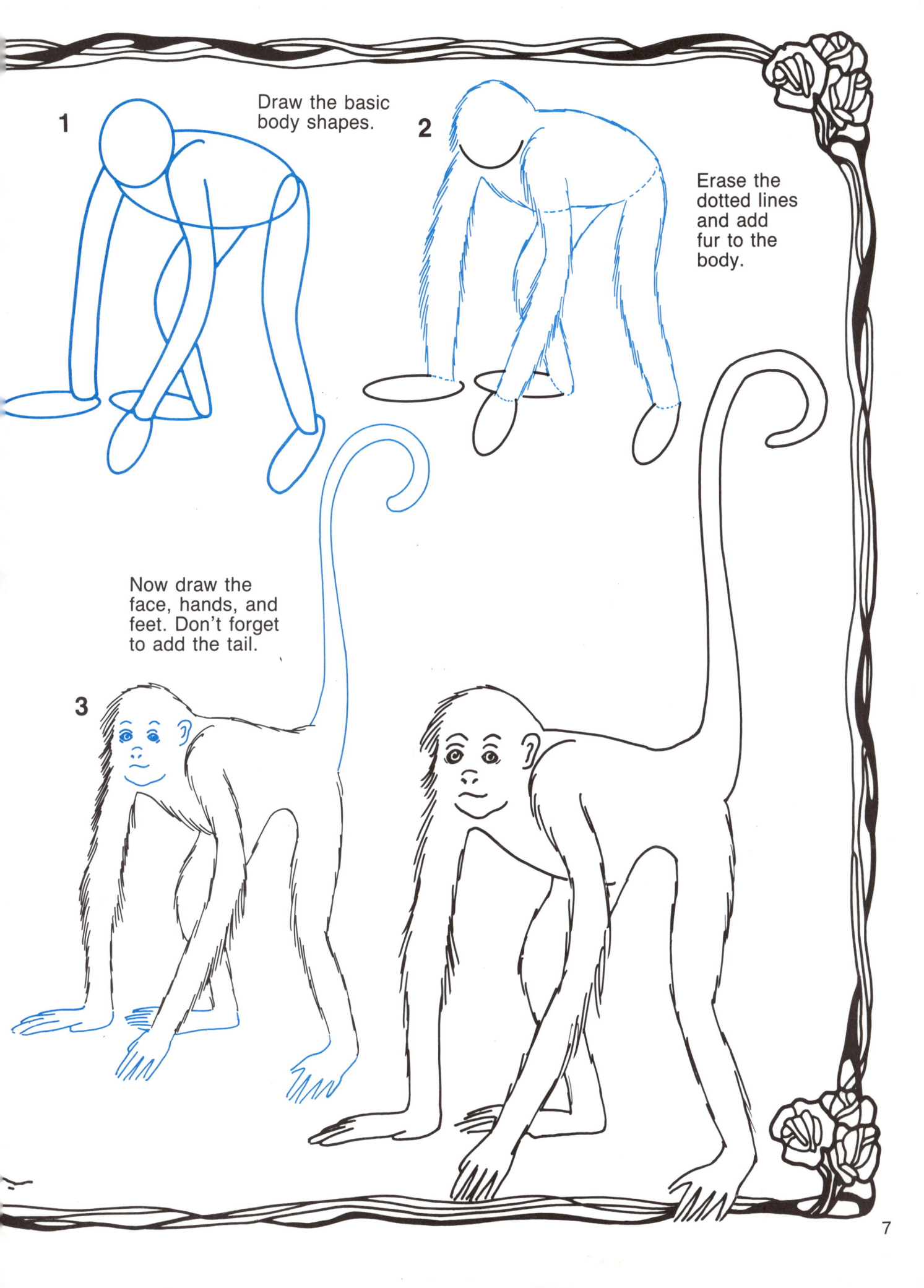

**2** Erase the dotted lines and add fur to the body.

**3** Now draw the face, hands, and feet. Don't forget to add the tail.

# Ape

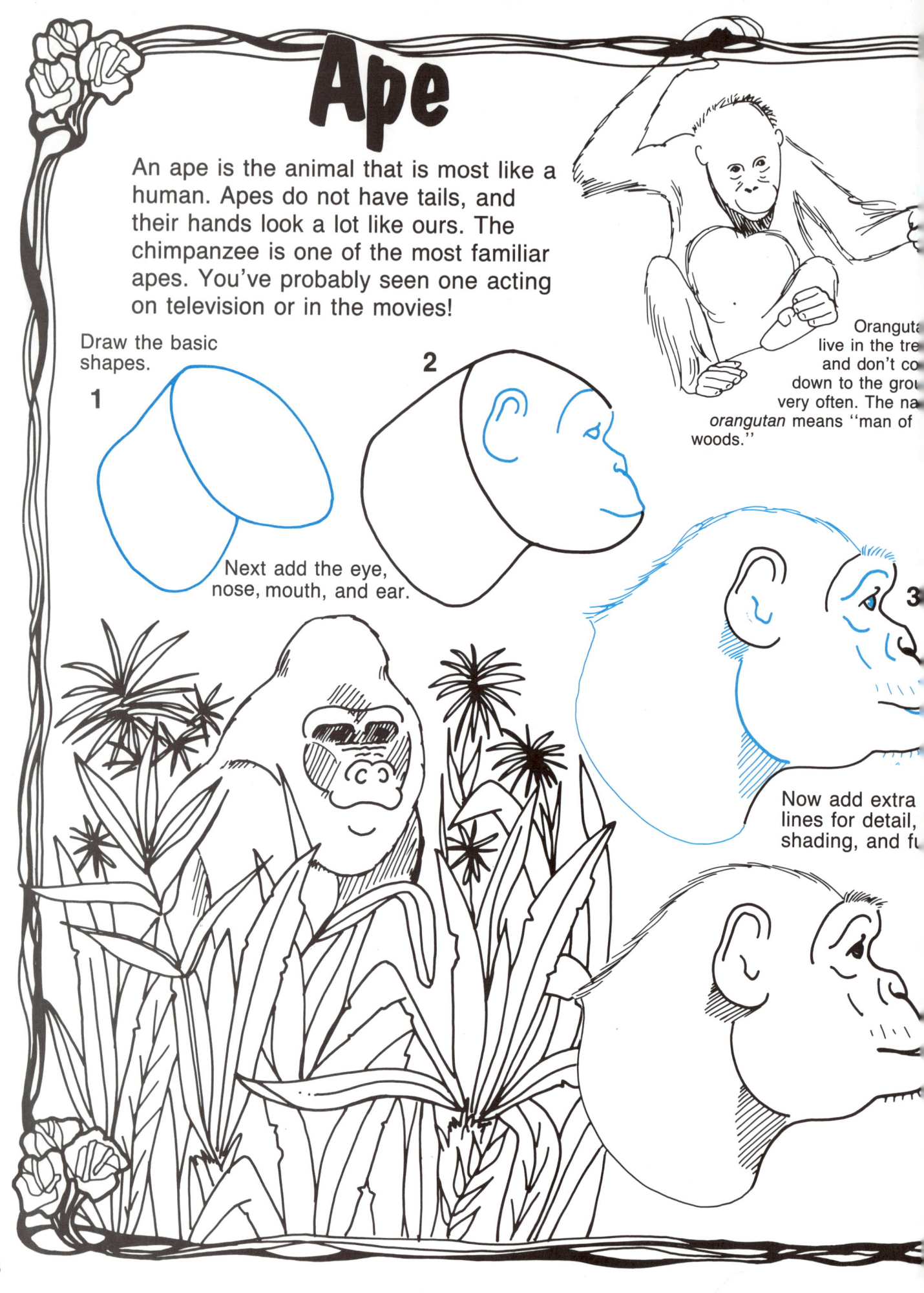

An ape is the animal that is most like a human. Apes do not have tails, and their hands look a lot like ours. The chimpanzee is one of the most familiar apes. You've probably seen one acting on television or in the movies!

Orangutan[s] live in the tre[es] and don't co[me] down to the gro[und] very often. The na[me] *orangutan* means "man of [the] woods."

Draw the basic shapes.

1

Next add the eye, nose, mouth, and ear.

2

3

Now add extra lines for detail, shading, and fu[r].

8

1. Draw the basic shapes.

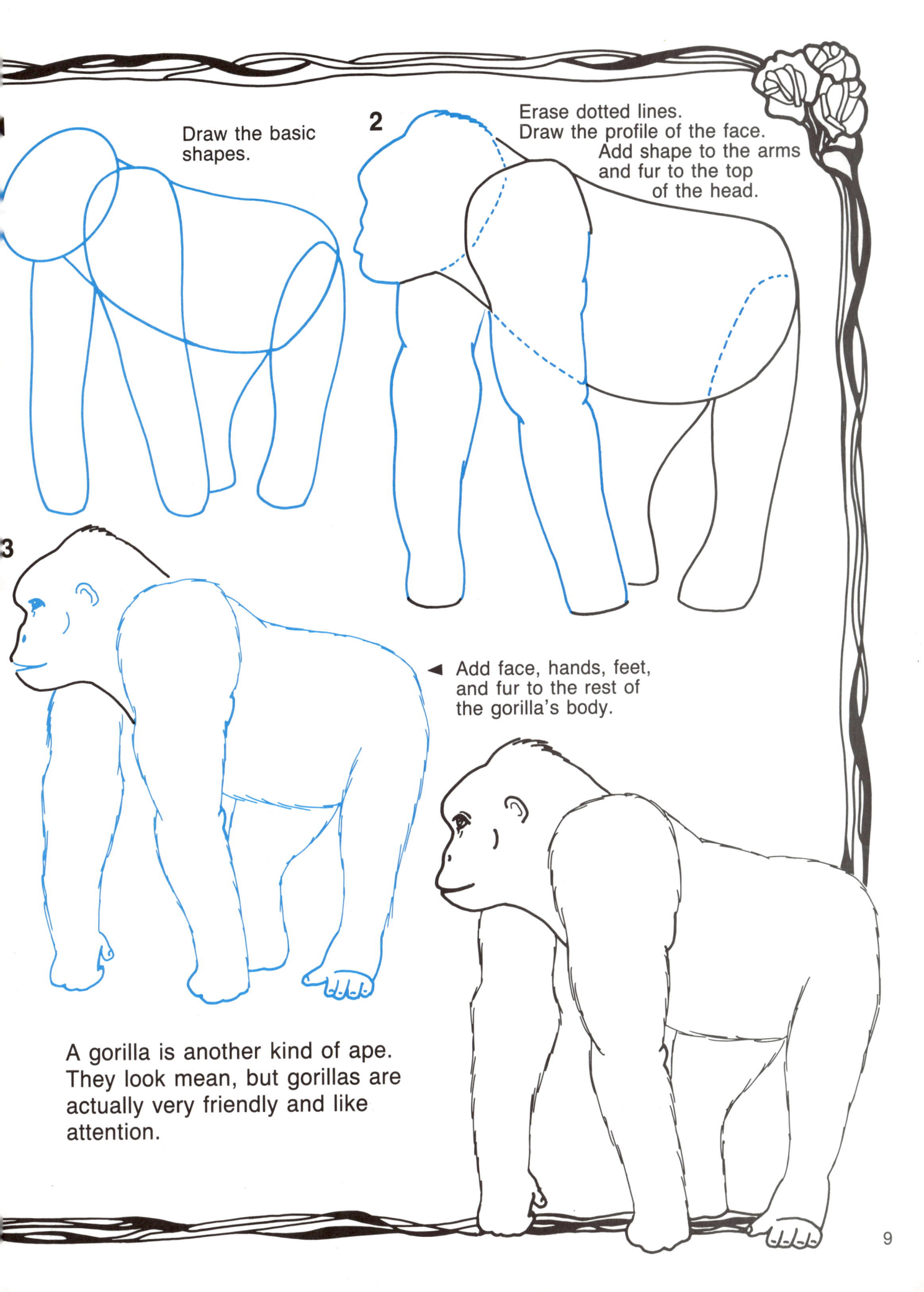

2. Erase dotted lines. Draw the profile of the face. Add shape to the arms and fur to the top of the head.

3. 

◀ Add face, hands, feet, and fur to the rest of the gorilla's body.

A gorilla is another kind of ape. They look mean, but gorillas are actually very friendly and like attention.

# Toucan

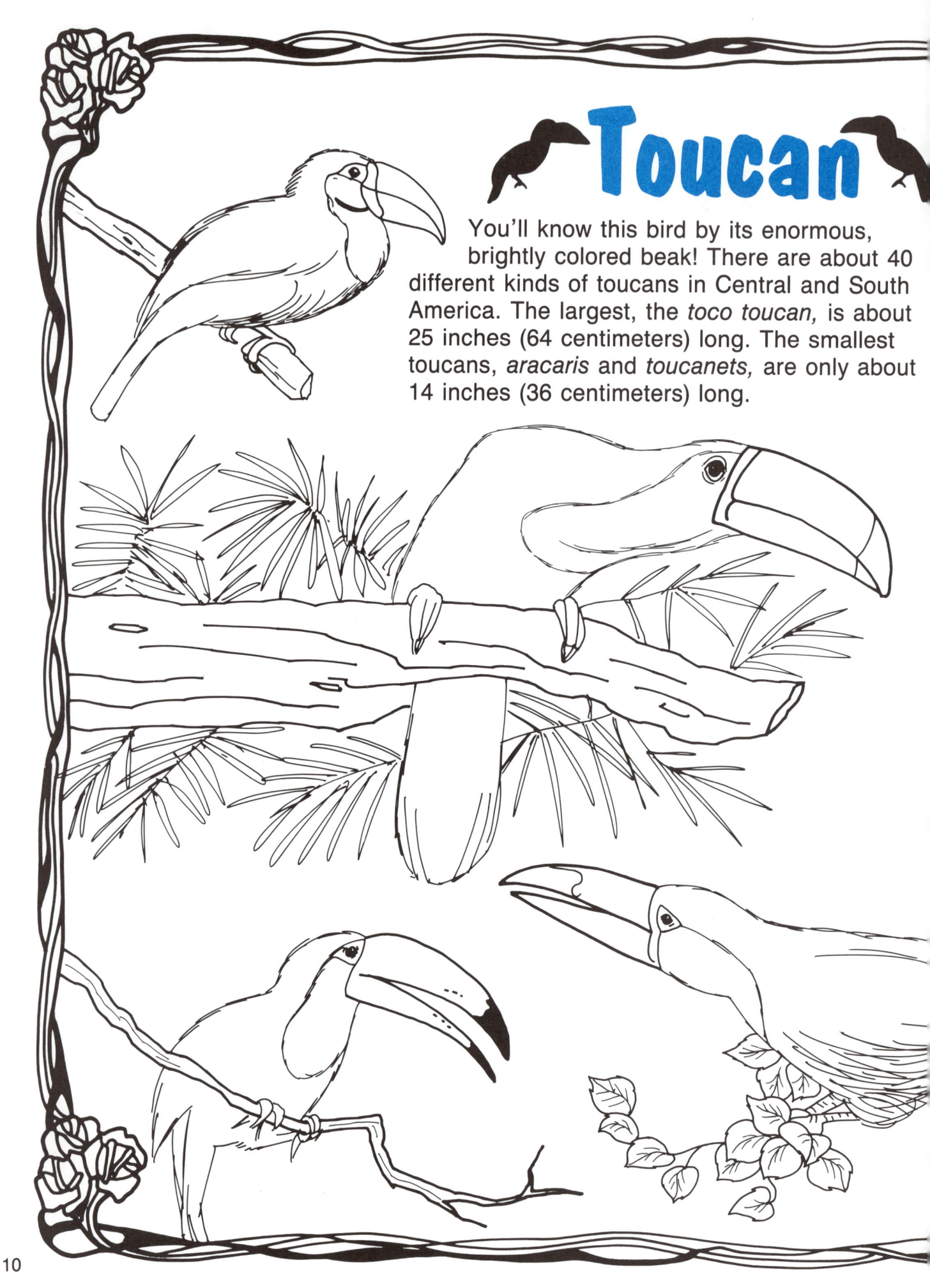

You'll know this bird by its enormous, brightly colored beak! There are about 40 different kinds of toucans in Central and South America. The largest, the *toco toucan,* is about 25 inches (64 centimeters) long. The smallest toucans, *aracaris* and *toucanets,* are only about 14 inches (36 centimeters) long.

**1** Draw the basic body shapes.

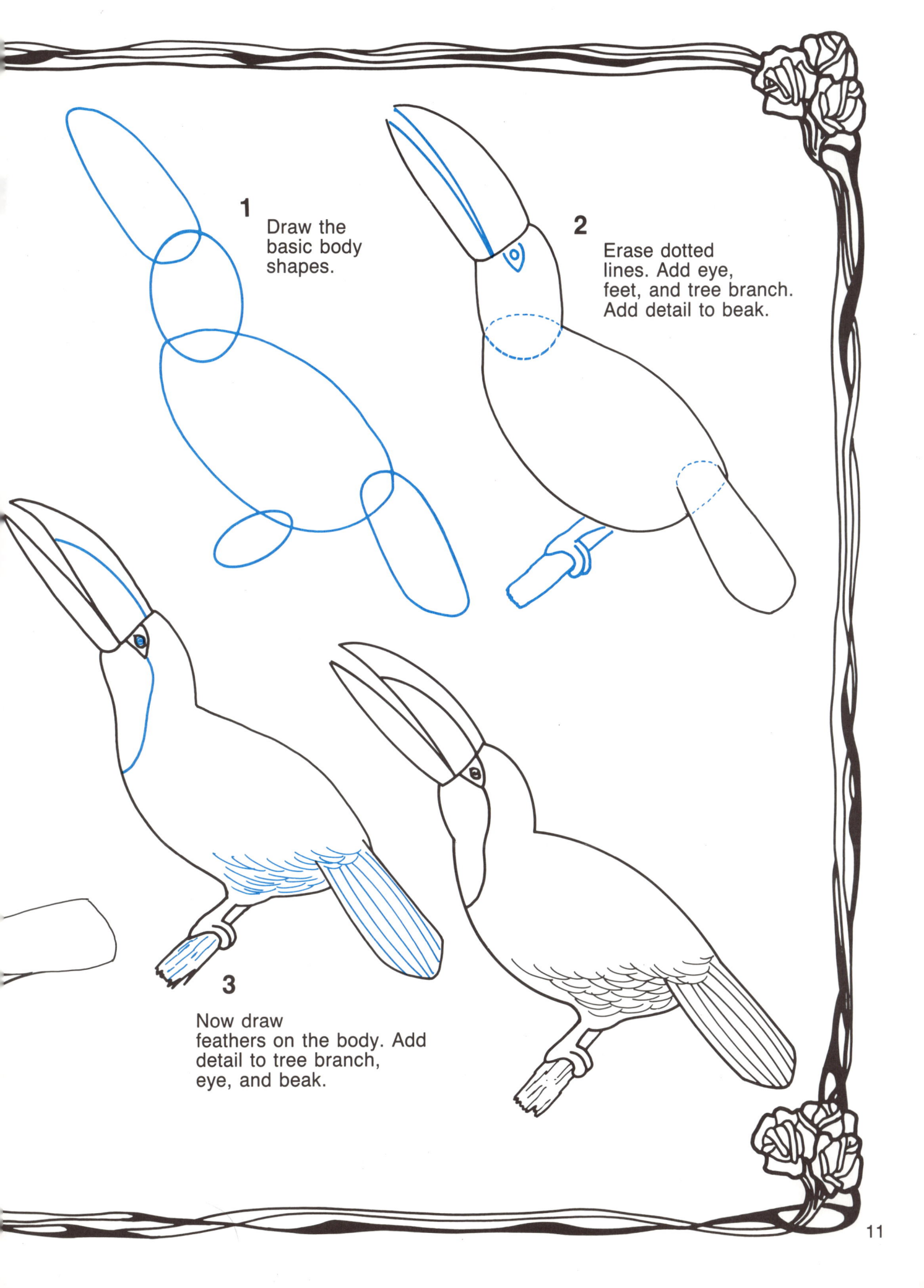

**2** Erase dotted lines. Add eye, feet, and tree branch. Add detail to beak.

**3** Now draw feathers on the body. Add detail to tree branch, eye, and beak.

11

# Lioness

A mother lion hunts for food, and teaches her cubs to protect themselves. Lion cubs are very playful. They stay close to their mothers until they are about two years old.

**1** Draw the basic shapes.

Erase dotted lines. Add detail to the face and shape to the legs. Don't forget the tail!

**2**

**3**

Now shade the face and body. Add detail to the tail.

# Lion

The mighty lion makes sure everyone knows he's King of the Beasts. These powerful animals live in groups called prides. The male lion has a collar of long, thick hair called a mane.

**1** Draw the basic body shapes.

**2** Draw the eyes, nose, mouth, ears, and tail. Add some hair under his mouth.

**3** Now add hair to the lion's mane. Draw eyes, and add detail to the feet.

# Rhinoceros

The word *rhinoceros* comes from two Greek words, and means "nose-horned." Some rhinoceroses have only one horn, while others have two. They use their horns for digging, and for defending themselves against other animals. There are 5 different kinds of rhinoceroses, but they are all nearly extinct.

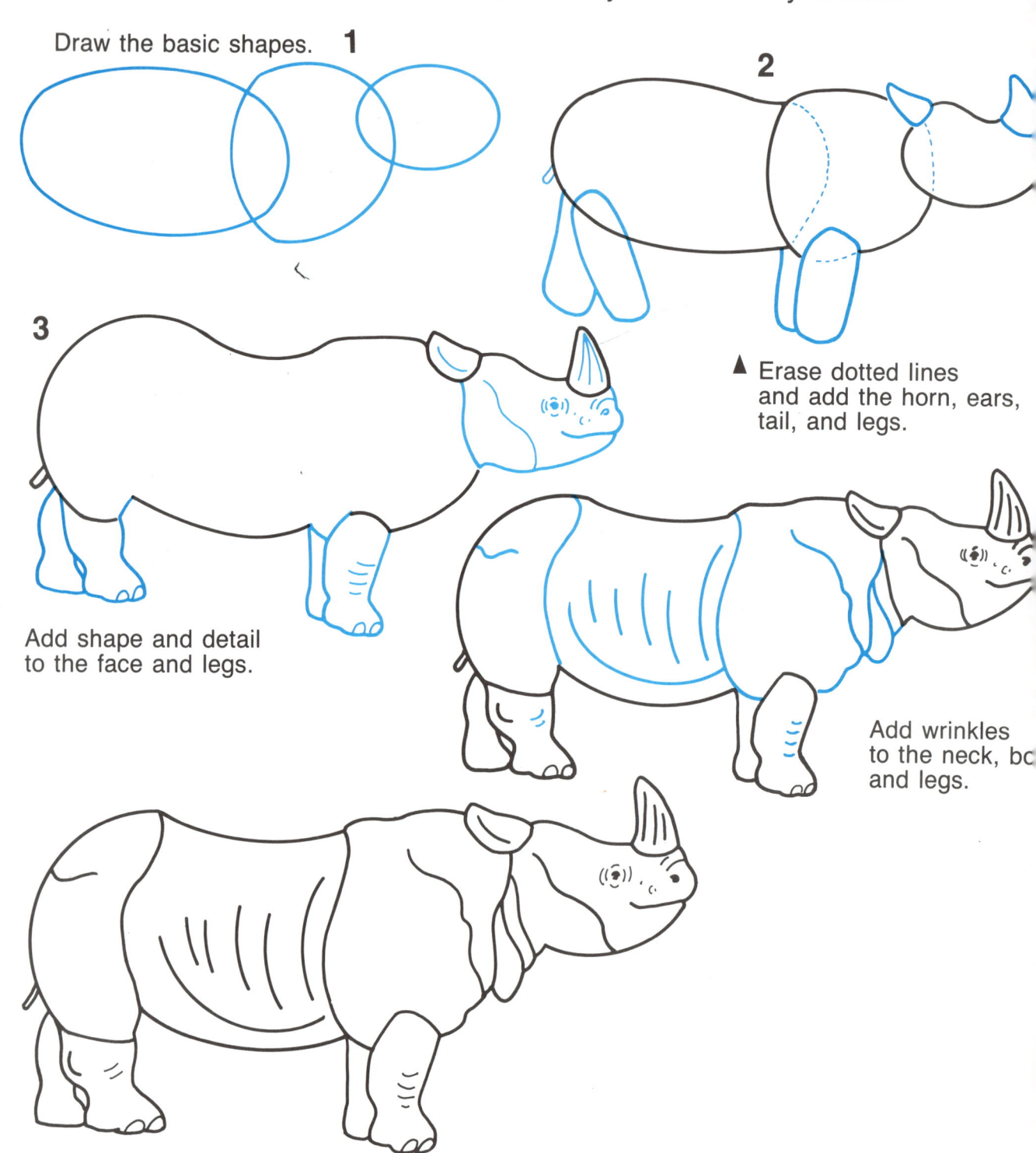

**1** Draw the basic shapes.

**2** Erase dotted lines and add the horn, ears, tail, and legs.

**3** Add shape and detail to the face and legs.

Add wrinkles to the neck, body and legs.

# Hippopotamus

You will find the hippopotamus in Africa, living close to the water. This animal has short legs and a huge head, and can weigh as much as 5,800 pounds (2,630 kilograms)! But the hippopotamus is a good swimmer and can run as fast as a human being. The word *hippopotamus* means "river horse."

**1** Draw the basic shapes.

**2** Erase dotted lines. Add the eye, nostril, mouth, ears, and legs.

**3** Now add detail to the face and feet. Draw wrinkles on the body.

17

# Zebra

A zebra looks a lot like a horse—except for its stripes! The stripes are white and black or dark brown, and help hide zebras from their enemies. Zebras live wild in Africa. They are hard to tame.

**1** Draw the basic body shapes. Be careful with the shape of the legs and hoofs.

**2** Erase the dotted lines. Draw in hair for the mane and tail. Add the eye, nostril, and ear. Also, add stripes to the tail.

**3** Add stripes to the body. You might want to include some shading for detail.

# Giraffe

The giraffe is the tallest animal on the Earth. Its legs are about 6 feet (2 meters) long, and its neck even longer.

Did you know that every giraffe has a different pattern on its furry coat?

It usually sleeps standing up. It is sometimes said that giraffes have no voices, but they can make soft sounds.

**1** Draw the basic body shapes.

**2** Erase dotted lines. Add the eye, nostril, ears, and horns.

**3** Now add the pattern to the face and body.

21

# Ostrich

The ostrich is the largest living bird. It sometimes grows to be 8 feet (about 2 and a half meters) tall! Ostriches have big brown eyes with very long eyelashes.

**1** Draw the basic shapes.

**2** Erase the dotted lines. Add the eye and mouth. Draw in legs and feet.

**3** Now add feathers and detail to the feet.

People think ostriches bury their heads in the sand when they are frightened, but this isn't true. They hide by sitting on the ground with their necks stretched out on the sand.

23

# Snake

A snake is a long, scaly reptile with no legs. It lives almost everywhere the world. There are about 2,700 different kinds of snakes. Some snake have poisonous bites, but not all of them are dangerous. The coral snak which is black, red, and yellow, is a poisonous snake that lives in North

**Cobra**

**Coral Snake**

**Python**

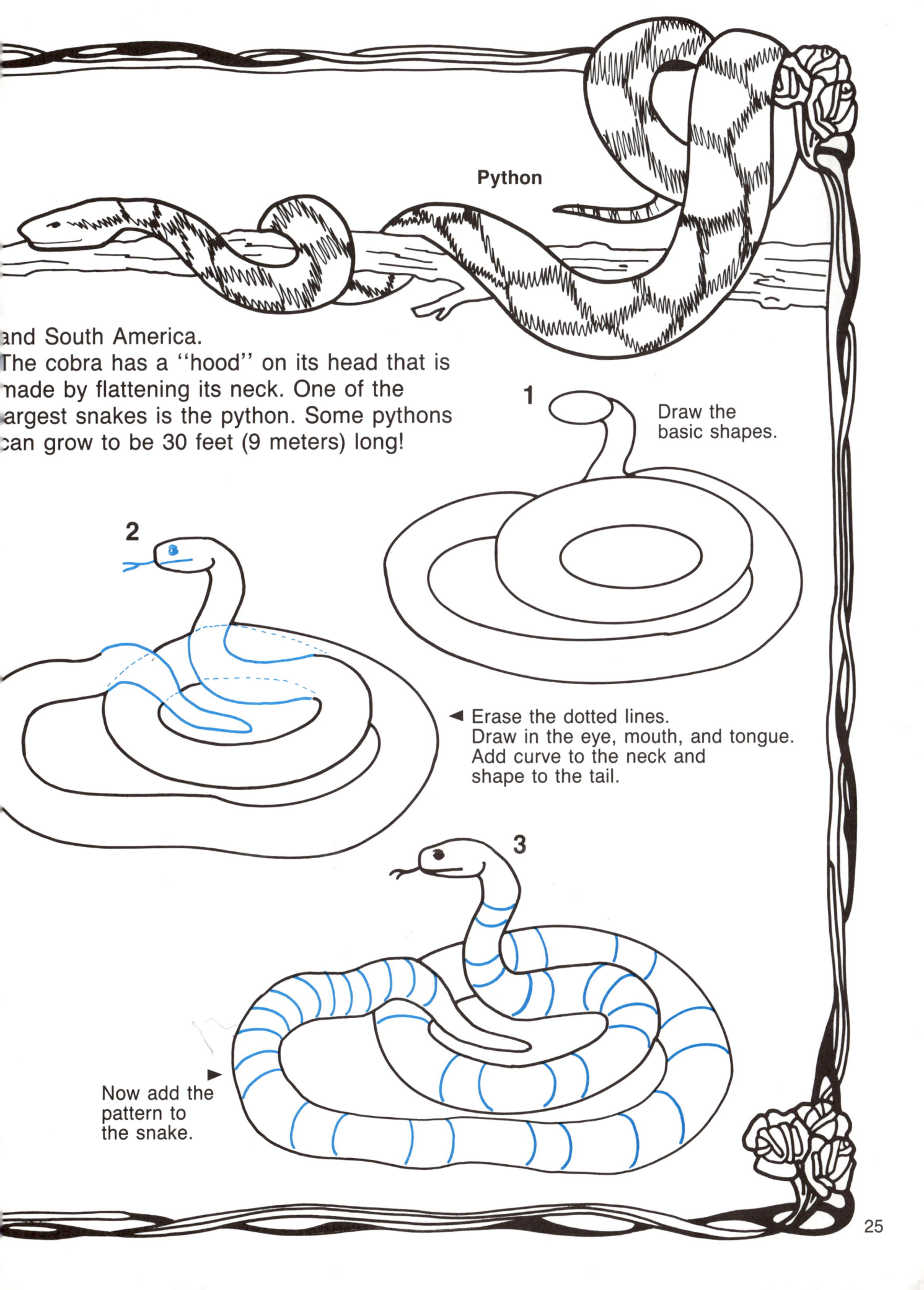

and South America.
The cobra has a "hood" on its head that is made by flattening its neck. One of the largest snakes is the python. Some pythons can grow to be 30 feet (9 meters) long!

**1** Draw the basic shapes.

**2** ◀ Erase the dotted lines. Draw in the eye, mouth, and tongue. Add curve to the neck and shape to the tail.

**3** ▶ Now add the pattern to the snake.

25

# Crocodile

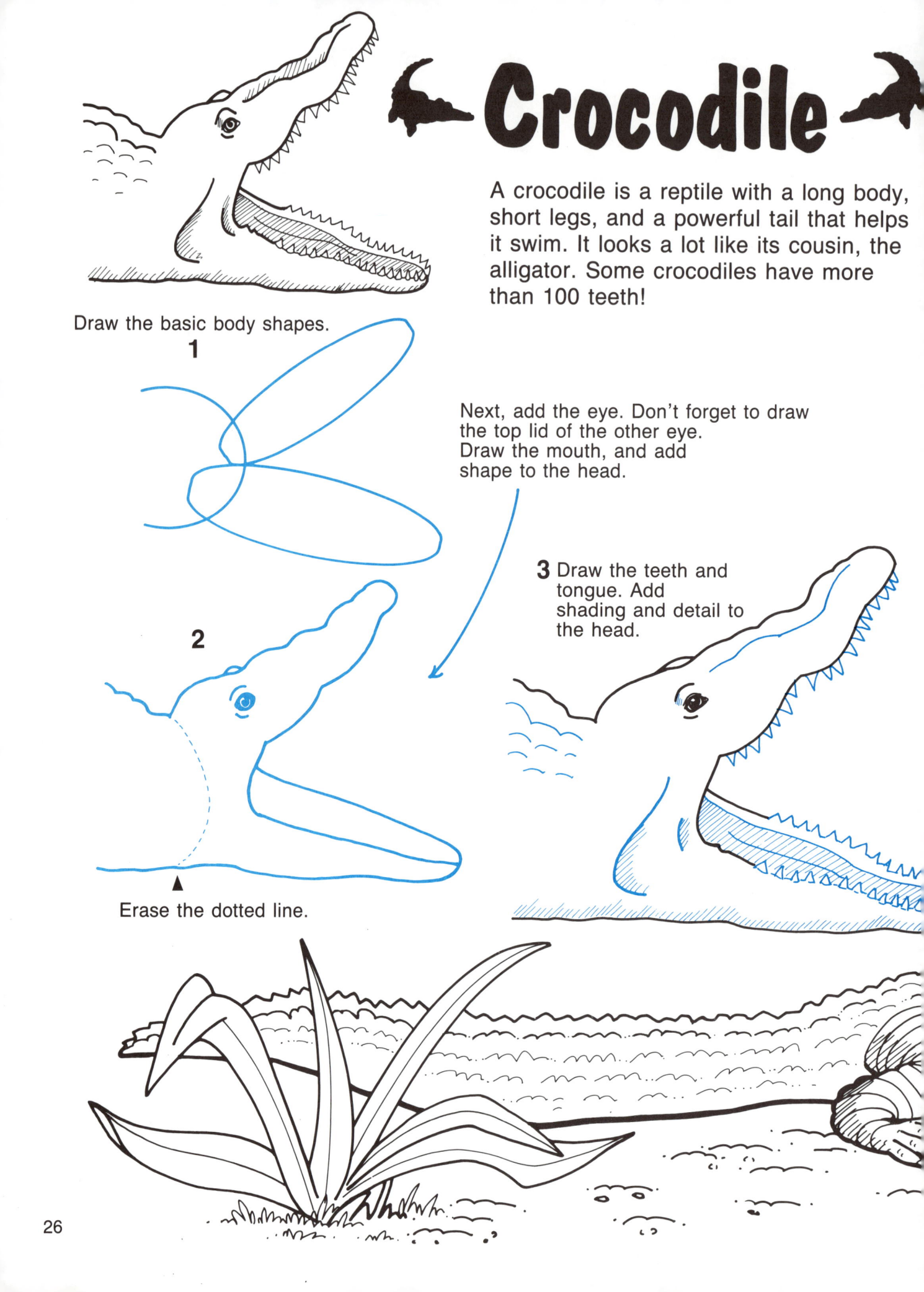

A crocodile is a reptile with a long body, short legs, and a powerful tail that helps it swim. It looks a lot like its cousin, the alligator. Some crocodiles have more than 100 teeth!

Draw the basic body shapes.

**1**

**2** Erase the dotted line.

Next, add the eye. Don't forget to draw the top lid of the other eye. Draw the mouth, and add shape to the head.

**3** Draw the teeth and tongue. Add shading and detail to the head.

1. Draw the basic shapes.

2. Erase the dotted line. Add the eye and mouth. Shape the legs and feet, and add detail to the back, all the way down to the end of the tail.

3. Add teeth. Draw bumps on the crocodile's body.

27

# Parrot

Parrots are brightly colored birds that live in warm, tropical places. Some people keep parrots as pets because they can be taught to talk.

Draw the basic shapes. Next, erase the dotted lines. Add shape to the body.

Draw in the eye, beak, feet, and tree branch. Now, add the feathers. Have fun!

28

The biggest parrots are called *macaws*. Macaws have long tails and blue, green, red, and yellow feathers.

# Tiger

The tiger is the largest mem[ber] of the cat family. Its roar ca[n] be heard for more than 2 m[iles] (3 kilometers)! Tigers can b[e] very dangerous. But most w[ild] tigers stay away from peo[ple] unless they are sick or [ ] hurt. Tigers can live i[n] almost any climat[e] although they are [ ] found only in Asia[.] Did you know tha[t a] tiger can leap alm[ost] 30 feet (9 meters)[?]

30

**1** Draw the basic shapes.

**2** Add the face and tail. Add shape to the body. Erase the dotted lines.

**3** Add shading and stripes.

31

# Gazelle

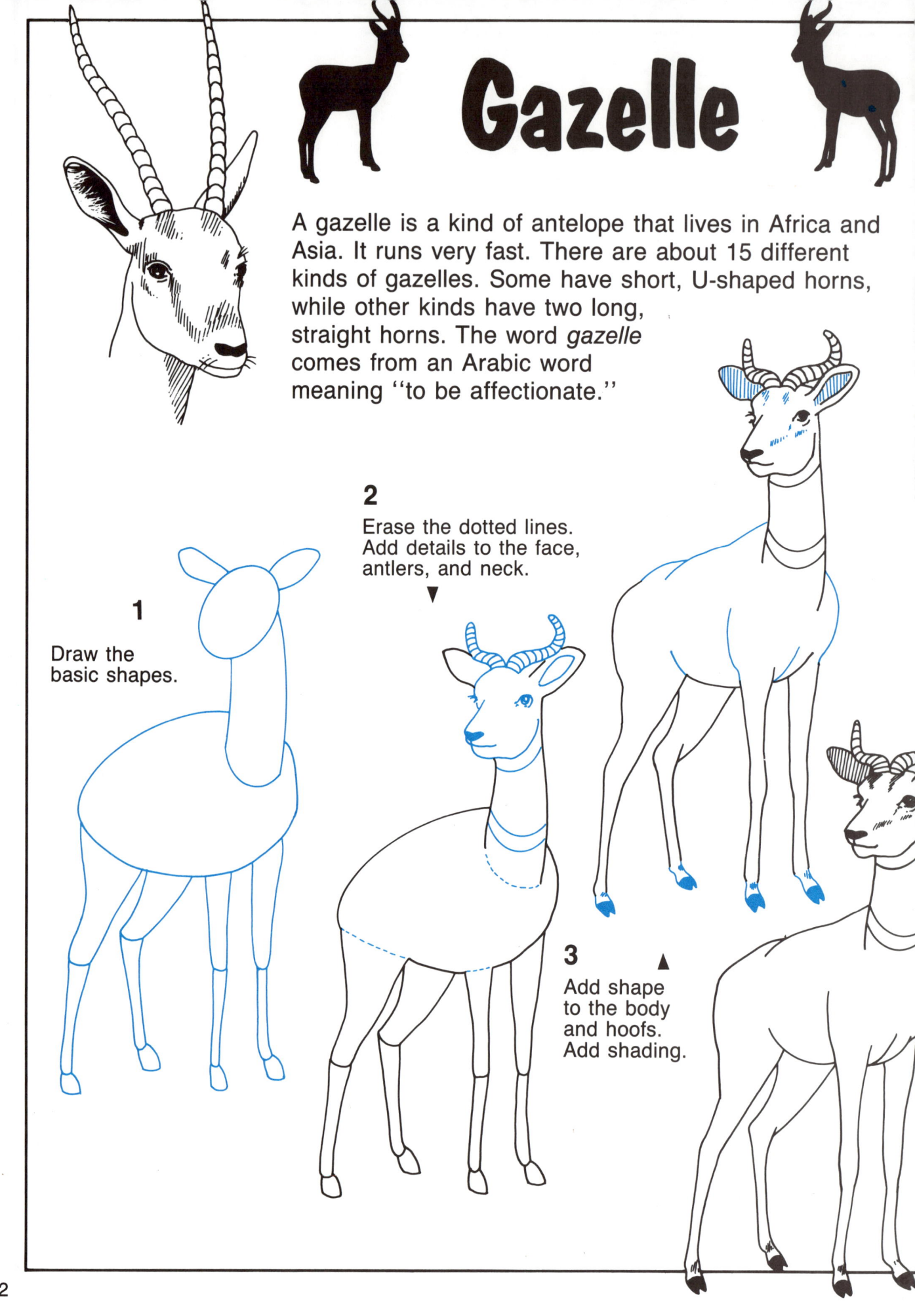

A gazelle is a kind of antelope that lives in Africa and Asia. It runs very fast. There are about 15 different kinds of gazelles. Some have short, U-shaped horns, while other kinds have two long, straight horns. The word *gazelle* comes from an Arabic word meaning "to be affectionate."

**1** Draw the basic shapes.

**2** Erase the dotted lines. Add details to the face, antlers, and neck.

**3** Add shape to the body and hoofs. Add shading.